THE GREAT SKATE GUIDE

Pull the Tricks. Live the Life.

Published in Great Britain in 2005 by Buster Books,
an imprint of Michael O'Mara Books Limited,
9 Lion Yard, Tremadoc Road,
London, SW4 7NQ, UK

A CIP catalogue record for this book is available from the British Library.

ISBN 1—905158-09-2

1 3 5 7 9 10 8 6 4 2

Printed and bound in Great Britain by Cox & Wyman, Reading, Berks

www.mombooks.com

Picture acknowledgements:
Cover image: Justin McManus / Rex Features
Robert Beck / Action Plus: pages 50 (top right), 64
Robert Beck / SI / Action Plus: page 60 (top)
Tim Leighton-Boyce / Action Plus: pages 49, 51, 54, 55
Getty Images: pages 50 (top left and below), 52, 53, 56, 57 (both), 58 (both), 59 (both), 60 (below right), 61 (both)
© Popperfoto.com: page 63 (below)
Neale Haynes / Rex Features: pages 62 (below), 63 (top)
George Konig / Rex Features: page 62 (top)
TopFoto.co.uk / IMW: page 60 (below left)
Picture research: Judith Palmer

THE
GREAT
SKATE
GUIDE

Pull the Tricks. Live the Life.

Buster
Books

contents

SKATER DATA 5

ONCE UPON A TIME 6

SKATE GEAR 13

LOVE YOUR BOARD 17

REGULAR OR GOOFY FOOT? 21

TRIX AND TIPS 22
    Grinds 46

PHOTO GALLERY 49

TRIX AND TIPS continued 65
    Slides 71
    Kerb Waxing 78
    Grabs 80
    Vert 82
    Old Skool 88

SKATE SPEAK 92

SKATER DATA

Skateboarding requires balance, nifty footwork and, of course, attitude, dude! It isn't just a fun, active and challenging sport – it's a way of life!

Whether you're a rookie or an old hand, a park or street rider, this book will help you learn lingo, master the moves and cut it as cool in one of the coolest cultures ever to exist.

Remember, though, that skating can be as dangerous as the next sport, so get quality gear, check it often and avoid broken bones.

Regular or goofy – get out there and ollie off!

The early days of skateboarding looked a bit like that scene in *Back To The Future*, with the little kids riding around on 2x4's with roller skates nailed to one side and a soap box screwed to the other. American kids in the 1930s grew tired of ordinary roller skates and decided to attach them to a plank of wood. These very basic 'boards' could not be directed or used for tricks. In the past seventy years, skating has had a habit of dying out and then re-emerging. However, it is always kept alive by the hardcore underground skaters...

1950: The introduction of 'trucks' (the device that holds the wheels), so that boards could be steered. Surfers took to the sport to keep themselves amused during 'flat wave days'. They would carve down hills like modern longboarders. At the time, skating was called 'Sidewalk' or 'Terra Surfing'.

1958: The first skateboards went on sale in a small surf shop in California. The shop owner, Bill Richards, made a deal with the 'Chicago Rollerskate Company' to produce skate wheels. The board was called the 'Roller Derby' and had clay wheels.

1963: The first real skate contest took place at a school in Hermosa, California, which really kicked things off.

1965: Skating hits the big time. The record 'Sidewalk Surfing' was released and a little later came the silent movie *Skater Dater*. The next Hermosa skate comp. was so big it even featured on ABC's *World Sports* programme, and soon it was on the cover of *Life* magazine, which called it 'the most exhilarating and dangerous joy-riding device this side of the hot rod'. Over fifty million skateboards were sold over a three-year period.

Then came the crash, skating lost its cool and began to die out. This wasn't just because of the over-hype but because skate companies were so busy churning out the boards, they didn't stop to evolve or improve them. The clay wheels were really slippery and caused hundreds of serious accidents and a few deaths, too. Cities began to ban skating and doctors labelled it 'the new medical menace'.

1970s: The first comeback. This was mainly down to two guys, Larry Stevenson of Los Angeles, who invented the 'kick tail', and Frank Nasworthy, who invented the polyurethane wheel with bearings. The seventies were called skateboarding's golden years. By 1975 there were over 300 parks in America and over forty million skateboards sold. Skaters started hitting empty swimming pools and getting their first tastes of vert. By 1978 the boards had become wider and fatter and some now had graphics on the board's darkside. Then came a huge moment in skateboarding history. In late 1978 a man called Alan 'ollie' Gelfand invented what is now known as the 'ollie', the move that virtually all modern-day tricks are based on. Suddenly skaters had the ability to jump over objects, giving the sport a giant leap away from its surfing origins.

Then skating died out again. Lawsuits followed injuries and cities began to ban it again (Norway outlawed skating completely). Skateparks had to pay huge insurance costs, so soon there was not a single park left open in California. Also, skating was taken over by the introduction of the BMX.

1981: Skating makes another comeback. *Thrasher* magazine, a guide for the underground skater, is first published and things slowly start to pick up.

1982: Tony Hawk won his first contest at the Del Mar Skate Ranch.

Mid-1980s: Vert riding took off in a big way, as did streetstyle skating. As well as Tony Hawk, classic cult skaters such as Lance Mountain, Mark Gonzales and Rodney Mullen dominated the scene. The first skate video *Bones Brigade* was released. New manufacturers appeared, like Powell Peralta, Vision/Sims and Santa Cruz, along with show companies, Airwalk and Vans. Soon skaters started competing for big money.

Late 1980s: The beginning of the 'New school', where technical tricks took centre-stage, led by the flatland king, Rodney Mullen. Skateboarders competed in freestyle, slalom, downhill, high and long jumping events. Pro skater Steve Rocco started up World Industries. Then skating took another nose-dive, this time because of worldwide recession.

1990s: Skating re-emerged in the early nineties. The emphasis this time was more on streetstyle. Companies came and went (many run by pro skaters), new technology and tricks were developed and new names emerged, until today's fun sport took shape.

SKATE GEAR

So, what do you need to take to the streets and the parks as a skater? First, the essentials:

THE SKATEBOARD:

Deck – made of laminated layers of plywood, with raised tail and nose

Grip tape – applied to top for traction and grip

Trucks x 2 – attached to underside of board with nuts and bolts to hold wheels; used for turning

Wheels x 4 – made of polyurethane; different wheels suit different surfaces

Mounting hardware – for obvious reasons

Precision bearings x 2 – inserted into each wheel, attached to the axle of the trucks with nuts; made for speed and durability

Completes: Pre-assembled complete set-ups are ideal for first-timers. They are made up of the same quality components, but come ready to ride.

PROTECTIVE GEAR:

Helmet, knee pads, elbow pads, and wrist guards.

IMPORTANT NOTE: ALWAYS BUY PRODUCTS MADE BY REPUTABLE BRANDS TO QUALITY STANDARDS. CHEAPER, LOW-GRADE PRODUCTS CAN OFTEN BE FAULTY AND UNSAFE. TAKE NO RISKS OUT THERE!

"WEARABLES" FOR THE LOOK:

Cool name-brand, flat-soled shoes
Short-sleeved tees
Long-sleeved hoodies
Baggy trousers, jeans or cargo pants
Beanies or caps

A pick of the top brand names:

Many of the companies sell skateboards, components, clothing and accessories. Baker, Birdhouse, Blueprint, Darkstar, Flip, Fury, Grind King, Independent, Lucky, Pig, Powell, Ricta, Speed Metal, Spitfire, Thunder, Tony Hawk, Variflex, Venture, World Industries, Zoo York.

Shoes and clothes: Chocolate, DC, Vans, Emerica, Etnies, Howies, Osiris, Volcom.

Other cool stuff: You can, of course, get a whole heap of wicked stuff to complete your look: key chains, watches, belts, visors, wallets, goggles, socks...the list goes on. How much do you want to spend?

LOVE YOUR BOARD

Skateboards are pretty straightforward objects and don't need much maintenance, but if you look after your board, it will look after you. Better to spend a few minutes checking your board than checking into Casualty!

Always carry a 'skate key'. This little tool will fix most of your problems.

DECK

When applying grip tape, don't cut round the edges – file the paper off with a wood file.

Use only downstrokes and then peel away the excess. This will prevent you from snagging or pulling up the grip tape. If your deck's covered in dirt and not gripping well, clean your grip tape with a stiff bristle brush and a little water.

Chips are the most common problem with decks. These happen when you wipe out and your board lands on either the nose or tail, and the wood splinters. The best thing is to keep a little sandpaper with you, so when this occurs you can smooth down the rough edges to prevent pulling up any more ply.

Pressure cracks are also common, but if your board is cracked badly and the layers of ply have begun to separate, it's time for a new purchase!

TRUCKS

The trucks are connected to the deck with four bolts each. Make sure these bolts are always tight. If they get loose, the trucks will rattle, the bolts will move in their holes and then they will never tighten properly again. Replace them if they seem at all dodgy.

Your kingpin is the steering bolt through the centre of the truck. Always carry a spare because when it goes, that's it. You'll need a skate key or a socket set and always keep an eye on your washers, etc. – they tend to walk.

Keep an eye on your bushings (rubbers) – they will wear out long before the trucks, but are cheap to replace from your local skate shop.

WHEELS

Check for flat spots on the wheels and always make sure your wheel bolts are tight – the last thing you want is to lose a wheel on the way down a set of eight.

Check your bearings. If they sound rough when you spin them, or if they pop out of the wheel too easily, then your bearings are worn, so get a fresh set.

REGULAR OR GOOFY FOOT?

Regular and goofy are the two different kinds of stance on the skateboard and are determined by whether you are stronger on your left or right foot. If you are equal on both, then you are a lucky dude because you'll be pulling off the switch tricks before anyone else.

Regular – When you skate with your left foot forward and your right foot on the tail of the board.

Goofy – When you skate with your right foot forward and your left foot on the tail of the board.

TRIX AND TIPS

Before learning any of these tricks you gotta get a feel for the board. Just ride on flat ground (flatland) whenever you get the chance, find your balance, practise carving and get used to spills.

All the tricks in this book have a star difficulty rating – the more stars, the harder the trick.

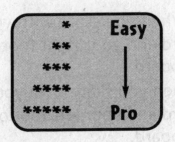

VARIAL *

This is the simplest trick you can do. All you do is jump 180 degrees and land back on your board. Use this move to add to existing tricks.

OLLIE ****

This is skating's most important trick and the one on which most other tricks are based. If you are a first-timer, you're gonna find this one pretty hard. Like with most of the tricks in this book, you just gotta keep practising.

Place your front foot just behind the front truck bolt, towards the middle of the board, and your back foot slightly over the edge of the tail.

Keep your weight on the balls of your feet, ready to jump. Practise crouching down, bending your knees, until you've got your balance.

Crouch down, then, as you jump up, slam (pop) the tail down hard with your back foot and slide your front foot towards the nose of the board with a slight downward pressure. This front-foot action will level the board in midair.

If you keep your shoulders parallel to the board, you should stay in a straight line. When you reach the peak of your ollie, put your weight equally on both feet. Keep your knees relaxed and slightly bent to land. When you land, your feet should be over the trucks. Ride on!

FAKIE OLLIE *

Obviously you gotta learn to ollie first. Any fakie trick means you have to be going backwards.

Keep your feet in the normal ollieing position, but you need to be rolling backwards.

MANUAL **

This is a basically a wheelie. The only difficulty is keeping your balance.

Place your front foot over the front truck bolts and put your back foot over the base of the tail. Just raise the nose and don't let your tail hit the ground.

OLLIE MANUAL **

The next stage in this trick is to ollie manual. Practise on low kerbs. Simply do a small ollie and land on your back two wheels, keep your balance, and manual away.

NOSE MANUAL ***

Nose manuals are the same as regular, but balancing on your front two wheels instead, which is a lot more difficult.

SHOVE-IT **

A trick performed by spinning the board 180 degrees beneath the feet while moving forward. Practise this trick standing still at first. Place your feet in the ollie position. As you pop the tail, bring your back foot down and pull it backwards, turning the board.

Keep your front foot clear until the board has spun through 180 degrees.

Catch the board with both feet at the peak of the trick. Bring it down, bending your knees.

BACKSIDE SHOVE-IT **

This is effectively the same as a normal shove-it, but the board spins anti-clockwise.

As you ollie, kick your back foot forwards, spinning the board in the opposite direction. Catch the board with both feet and land it.

360 SHOVE-IT ***

This is similar to the shove-it, except the board turns 360 degrees.

Place your feet in the ollie position, but put your back foot nearer the toe-side of the tail.

As you pop the tail, kick your back foot backwards, hard enough to spin the board 360 degrees.

Make sure you keep your front foot out of the way. When the board has finished rotating, catch it with your back foot, and land it, bending your knees.

FRONTSIDE 180 **

This trick involves you and the board turning 180 degrees in the air together, with the front of your body leading. You must learn to ollie first.

Place your front foot three-quarters of the way up the board and your back foot on the centre of the tail.

Start with the normal ollieing motion, but kick your back foot behind you, and at the same time slide your front foot up the board and push the nose forwards. This will turn the board 180 degrees, and hopefully you with it.

If successful, you will land fakie and ride away.

BACKSIDE 180 **

The same as the frontside but, when you are turning, your back is leading so you are spinning 180 degrees in the opposite direction.

When in the ollie position, place your back foot nearer the heel-edge of the board.

When you ollie, push your back foot forwards and your front foot back.

The trick is to keep both feet on the board while turning in the air.

KICKFLIP ***

This trick involves spinning the board 360 degrees through the air like a torpedo before landing back on it.

Place your feet in the ollie position, but place your front foot so it is only covering the back two bolts of the front truck and is slightly towards the heel-side of the board.

Pop the tail and slide the front foot up and towards the heel-side of the board. When it hits the concave on the edge of the board, kick out and downwards at the same time. This will cause the board to spin.

Once the board has made a full rotation, catch it with your back foot, then add the front foot to stabilize the board and bring it down to the ground.

Land with your feet over the truck bolts, bend your knees and roll away.

DOUBLE FLIPS AND TRIPLE FLIPS ****

The same as a kickflip, but with more rotations. You need to get more air and flip the board harder.

HEELFLIP ***

Similar to the kickflip, but the board rotates the other way and you spin the board with your heel as opposed to the front of your foot.

Start in the ollie position, but place your front foot so that your toes are over the edge of the side of the board.

Do the same motion as the kickflip, but as you drag your foot up the board, drag it towards the toe-side of the board.

When your heel makes contact with the concave, kick out and downwards. This will spin the board.

Catch the board with your back foot. Add the front foot to stabilize and land it while bending your knees.

SEX CHANGE **

This is a good trick to follow the kickflip, however most people tend to miss the difference. The sex change is basically a kickflip while doing a body varial, so you land fakie.

Get into the normal kickflip position with your back foot in the middle of the tail and your front foot halfway up the board and slightly to the heel-side.

Pop the tail hard and do a kickflip, but

this time get your body higher off the ground so you can turn yourself 180 degrees in the air.

You need to land with your feet over the truck bolts. If you have pulled the trick off correctly, then you should be riding away fakie.

THE BIG SPIN ****

This is simply a 180 body varial over a 360 shove-it. However, you are turning in the opposite direction to the board.

Stand as if you were going to do a kickflip with your front foot slightly towards the heel-side of the board.

Start as if you were doing a backside 180 but, as you pop the tail with your back foot, pull your back foot backwards to perform the 360 shove-it.

Turn your 180 backside in the air over your board, which should be 360 shove-iting in the opposite direction.

As you and the board are spinning, try to keep your front foot hovering over the middle of the board. This will prevent the board from flipping and enable you to catch it.

Once you and the board have stopped spinning, it's time to catch the board. You should have your feet in the backside landing position with each foot over the truck bolts.

Apply pressure to stop the board spinning, slam the board to the ground and ride away.

SHOVE-IT FLIP (VARIAL FLIP) ****

This trick is the combination of a shove-it and a kickflip. So, as the board is turning 180 degrees, it is also doing a full flip at the same time.

Place your feet in the kickflip position with your front foot over the truck bolts, but nearer to the heel-side of the deck and your back foot near the toe-side of the tail.

Pop the tail down and backwards to start the shove-it.

Just as the front end of the board begins to move away from you, slide your foot up the board and towards the heel side of the deck, and when it reaches the concave, kick down and outwards, but make sure you don't flip it too hard or you'll stop the board from shove-iting.

You will find, as the board turns, your front foot will be drawn into a kickflip anyway.

Keep both feet well clear of the board while it's spinning.

When the board has finished spinning, catch it with your back foot. Land it and ride away.

SALL FLIP *****

This is one of those annoyingly difficult tricks which can cause you plenty of pain. So, if you like that kind of thing, this is the trick for you.

Start in the ollie position, but hold your leading hand out in front of you, with your palm facing down and your fingers pointing towards your body.

Now you have to ollie and catch the nose of the board with your hand, making sure your fingers are on top of the grip tape.

Once you have a firm grip on the board, you have to spin the board in a 360 shove-it motion underneath you, but don't let go of the nose.

Once the board has completed its spin, place it back underneath you, let go of the nose and land it (do not try to do more than a 360 unless you are freaky).

360 FLIP *****

Like a shove-it flip, but the board turns 360 degrees instead of 180 degrees while flipping. The secret of this trick is getting enough air, in order to complete the trick before landing it, so if you're still not getting good air, you should practise plenty of ollies first.

Get into the kickflip position, but place your back foot more towards the toe-side of the tail.

Pop the tail hard and at the same time sweep your back foot behind you. Slide your front foot up the board towards the heel-edge, flipping the board when it has turned about 45 degrees.

Keep your feet clear of the board, but try to keep them level with your shoulders. When the board has spun 360 degrees, catch it with the back foot first. Land, bending your knees, and ride on.

CABALLERIAL *****

Named after pro-skater Steve Caballero, this trick is a fakie, frontside, 360. You and the board turn 360 degrees with the front of your body leading, while rolling backwards on the skateboard.

Start by pushing off fakie and get into the 180 ollie position with your front foot three-quarters of the way up the board.

Pop the tail hard and push it behind you at the same time. Slide your front foot up the board and towards the toe-side. This will start the board turning in the frontside direction.

The trick to pulling this off involves height and your arms. Swinging your arms will help you turn more in the air.

Turn as quickly and as smoothly as possible.

If you pulled it off, you should land fakie and ride away.

PRESSURE FLIP *****

This involves pulling off a kickflip, but using your back foot to spin the board.

Start in the normal ollie position. Do a straightforward ollie, sliding your front foot up to stabilize the board.

When in midair, kick your back foot down and behind you off the heel-side edge of the tail. As the board spins, make sure you keep both feet well clear.

Catch the board with both feet, land, and ride on.

SHIFTY *

If you mess up this trick, you tend to catapult off. A 'shifty' is like an indecisive 180. You start to turn, but in midair you change your mind and turn back again.

Simply start by doing a 180. You should have turned the board as much as you want to by the time you hit the peak of the ollie. Then simply turn the board back again, land as in a normal ollie and ride away.

Warning: backside shifties tend to be a lot more difficult, so start with little shifts only.

HARDFLIP *****

This trick is a 180-degree back flip through the skater's legs and a half kickflip combined.

Start this trick as if you were doing a normal kickflip, by popping the tail and dragging your front foot up the board and towards the heel-side.

Make sure, as you flip the board, you flip it with your front foot nearer the nose than normal – this will give you a wide stance, allowing the board to back-somersault between your legs. A mistake here could cost you dearly.

At the same time, use your back foot to push the tail down and forwards so the board begins to backflip.

Your back foot needs to make a

circular motion in order not to hit the board, and keep your front foot well clear too.

Catch the board with either your front or back foot, whichever feels easier. Bring the board down to land and ride away.

IMPOSSIBLE *****

Called impossible for a very good reason. However, once you've mastered it, you'll be the Don at your local park.

The easiest way to start is with your front foot right up at the nose and your back foot hanging off the edge of the tail. You don't need to be going at a huge speed – the slower, the easier.

You don't want to pop the tail hard,

just bring it down so your shoe momentarily makes contact with the ground.

At the same time, lift your front foot clear of the board to keep it out of the way.

With your back foot, push the tail forwards so the board begins to backflip. The trick is to keep your back foot in contact with the tail at all times, so that the board pivots around your foot. As the board spins, it should be slightly on its side so that it does not hit the ground too easily.

After it has rotated, bring your back foot back and stop the spinning with your front foot.

Level up and land the board.

GRINDS

50-50 GRIND *

Move up to the obstacle and get in the ollie position (waxed kerb, rail, ledge).

When you are parallel to the obstacle, ollie so that both your trucks land on it at about the same time.

Keep your legs slightly bent while you're grinding – this helps with your balance.

At the end of your grind, pull up your nose into a manual to help you drop off. N.B. If you are facing the obstacle that you are grinding on, then it's frontside. If your back is towards the object, then it's backside.

5-0 GRIND **

Learn the 50-50 first. The 5-0 is a manual roll grind on the back truck. This grind's smoother and easier with a little more speed.

Start rolling up to your obstacle, with your feet in the ollie position. Come up parallel to the obstacle and ollie.

As you are landing on the kerb, push your tail down so that you land on the back hanger of your trucks only.

Now use your arms to balance you as you grind.

As you come to the end of your grind, give the tail a little pop, land on the ground and ride away.

SALAD GRIND **

Learn to 5-0 first. This trick is basically a 5-0, but you turn the board slightly away from the kerb.

Approach the obstacle in the standard ollie position.

When you ollie, turn the board about 25 degrees away from the kerb.

Put a little pressure on the tail, so you land with the back hanger on the kerb and with the nose of the board pointing away from the kerb.

When you finish the grind, give the tail a slight pop and straighten the board before you land.

Bowl jumping

Nose grab

Grinding on the halfpipe

Heel flip

Hand plant

Big air

Bigger air

Inverted aerial stunt

Watch out for a wipeout!

Awesome!

Tail grab

Toe flip

Tail grind

Nose grind

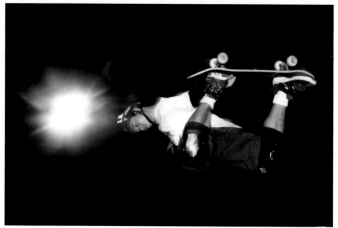

Left-handed grab

Right-handed grab

Jumping obstacles

Ollie off!

Street skating

Extreme ramp

Ultimate bowl

Old skool

Skateboard sledging

Mountain skateboarding

Motorized skateboarding

Big night air

NOSE GRIND****

Basically a 5-o grind on the front hanger or a nose manual roll grind. This trick needs lots of speed. So, go faster!

Roll up parallel to the kerb in the ollie position.

Pop the tail and ollie. As you are ollieing, slide your front foot right up the curve or the nose and apply pressure so the board is coming down nose-first. Land the front hanger of the truck on the kerb and grind.

The hard part is keeping your balance. As you are grinding, your front foot should be on the nose and your back foot around the back truck bolts. Also use your arms to stabilize yourself.

As you reach the end of your grind,

drop your tail hard while taking the weight off the nose – this will level the board. Land and ride away.

SMITH GRIND ****

This is similar to the salad, but while grinding on the back hanger, the front end of the board should face away from the obstacle and be pointing downwards below the level of the back hanger.

Pick up some good speed towards the kerb until you are rolling parallel to it.

Like the salad grind, pop an ollie and turn the board about 25 degrees away from the kerb.

Here comes the hard part: you should land as if you were going to do a 50-50, but the front truck is going to miss the kerb and go below the grinding line. Use your tail to control how low the nose goes (too low and you've blown it).

Use a combo of your arms and your tail foot to keep balance.

Pop the tail slightly, level the board, land and ride away.

CROOKED GRIND (K GRIND) *****

This trick's based on the 50-50 and the nose grind and is really difficult. It's a nose grind with the tail end of the board pointing away from the kerb.

Get up some speed and roll parallel with the kerb, with your feet in the ollie position.

Pop the tail and slide your foot further off the board so it's over the nose.

Land on the front hanger with your back leg half-bent, so you are in the nose manual position.

Almost as soon as the board begins to grind, push your back foot forwards, putting the board at a 25-degree angle.

It's easier to stay stable if your nose is actually making contact with the kerb. However, this will slow you down, so make sure you get a good speed up before the trick.

As you reach the end of the grind, lift your weight off the nose and at the same time pop a little pressure on the tail. This will lift up the nose, enabling you to straighten up the board and land smoothly.

FEEBLE GRIND ****

This is a mix between a 50-50 and a
board slide; or a smith grind with the
front end of the board pointing away
from the kerb in the opposite direction,
so that the darkside of the board makes
contact with the kerb, too.

Get up some speed and roll up parallel
to the kerb.

Pop an ollie as if you were going to do
a 50-50 but 'shifty' the nose frontside
about 25 degrees, so that you land with
the rear hanger grinding and the front
hanger hanging over the front of the
kerb. The darkside of the board should
be making contact and sliding, too.

If you put too much pressure on the
front end of the board, you will stall; too

much pressure on the tail and you will be doing a 5-0.

As you reach the end of the grind, pull off a gentle pop of the tail, straighten out your board and ride away.

SLIDES

To make them easier to explain, all these tricks are described on a flatland bar.

BOARD SLIDE *

This is the easiest of the slides, but can also lead to sack tapping if done incorrectly, so beware.

Most people find the board slide easier to do backside, so you are sliding with your back towards the end of the bar. Start by riding up to the bar parallel, so the bar is in front of you. Make sure your feet are in the frontside position.

Pop the tail and turn the board 90

degrees towards the bar and, at the same time, balance your feet so that they are parallel on the board. This will stop you from putting too much weight on any one side of the board.

Land the board gently (so as not to snap it) over the centre of the bar. Slightly bend your legs as you land, to help with your balance, and turn your head, so you can see where you're going.

As you reach the end of the bar, you can either continue turning the board frontside, so you land fakie, or turn the board back 90 degrees backside, so you ride away regular.

NOSE SLIDE **

Ride up parallel to the bar, so that it is facing your back.

Ollie and turn the board backside until the nose is over the bar.

As you ollie, slide the front foot up the board to the nose, so that when the nose is over the bar, you can apply pressure with your front foot, holding the nose to the bar.

Then simply slide a while.

When you hit the end of the slide, pull your body and your back foot backwards and at the same time push your front foot forwards, straightening out the board. Land and ride away.

TAIL SLIDE ***

Like a nose slide, but on your tail.

Ride up parallel to the bar, with the front of your body facing the bar.

Get your feet into the backside ollie position and do a backside 90, using your rear foot to bring the tail onto the bar.

When your tail hits the bar, put weight on your back foot and slide.

While sliding, don't lean too far forwards or backwards – tails are slippery things.

When you reach the end of the slide, pull your back foot backwards, straightening out the board. Land with bent knees and ride away.

BLUNT SLIDE ✳✳✳

This trick involves sliding with the board standing up vertically, with your wheels on the top of the bar and the tail touching the bar sides.

Ride up parallel to the bar and prepare to ollie.

Pop the tail and slide the front foot high up the board, at the same time turning the board 90 degrees and using your back foot to push the tail down, so that the board lands with your rear wheel on top of the bar and your tail touching the side of the bar.

Lean backwards a little – as this trick doesn't slide too easily, this will help push the slide along.

Once you have reached the end of the

slide, start turning the nose of the board downwards – this will give you more movement to pop the tail. Then pop the tail and level the board and land.

CASPER SLIDE *****

This move is mighty tricky, but looks darned good when you pull it off. It's a half flip slide, so you are sliding with the darkside of the board facing upwards.

Ride up so that the bar is parallel to you and you are facing it.

Get into the kickflip position.

Start the kickflip and, at the same time, turn the board frontside about 25 degrees.

As soon as the board turns a half flip, catch the board with your front foot underneath the front of the board (remember, the board should be upside-down, so the top of your foot is touching the grip tape) and your back foot on top of the underside of the tail.

The bar should touch the board in the middle and slide. Use your front and back feet to stabilize the board.

When you reach the end of the slide, pull your front foot backwards and up, so that it half flips the board again, and catch it with your rear foot.

Level out the board, land and ride on.

KERB WAXING

First to consider is your choice of wax. You can now buy wax made by skate companies like Powell. These are fast and easy to apply, but can cost a lot. Still the best of the best are your standard cheap household candles. These are great for waxing but, because of their shape, they tend to break into pieces or cause you to get knuckle rubs.

A good trick is to throw a few candles in a pan, melt them down and pour them into an unwanted pint glass. When the wax is dry, smash the glass (under controlled circumstances), and cut it into small pill-shaped pieces. The wax is now easier to use and won't crumble.

Another thing you can do is throw a couple of crayons into your melted wax to give those kerbs a hint of colour.

When waxing kerbs, always look out for gaps or chips in the stone – make sure these are well filled in with wax. Don't just wax the edge, put a big thick coat along the tops and sides, too. When you've done a coat, use your foot to pack down the wax until you can feel it becoming more slippery.

Remember there are a few people out there who don't appreciate the art of waxing, so stay sharp! It's a good idea not to wax kerbs on streets where old people live – they gave up skating a long time ago, and don't want to be forced to start again!

GRABS

INDY

Grabbing the right side of the board while making air.

AIRWALK

Holding the nose of the board while putting your front leg forwards and your back leg backwards (so it looks like you're walking).

TAIL GRAB

Grabbing the tail of the board while in the air.

BENNIHANNA

Sliding your ollie foot off the back of the board and letting it hang down while grabbing the tail.

ROCKET AIR

While getting big air, sliding your front foot to the centre of the board and grabbing the nose with both hands.

STALEFISH

Grabbing the heel-side of your board through your legs while in the air.

UERT

PERIMANIA

PUMPING *

This is the action that gets up your speed on a ramp. It helps to be able to drop in first, but if you can't do that yet, you can start from the bottom of the ramp.

First, get your feet into your most comfortable and stable position, and start by pushing towards one end of the ramp.

The trick to building up your speed is pressure from your knees. As you are going up, straighten your legs, taking your weight off the board and, as you come back down, bend your knees, pushing the board back down with your feet.

When riding the ramp, try to stay level with the board at all times, as if you were on flatland. If you lean too far forwards or backwards, then you'll wipe out.

Keep pumping at either side of the ramp until you are coming up to the coping.

DROPPING IN **

This is how you start your vert session, by dropping off the top of the ramp to the bottom.

Standing at the top of the ramp for the first time is pretty daunting, but you have to overcome that fear!

Place the tail of the board over the edge of the coping, so that the rest of the board is hovering over the ramp. Pin the tail there with your back foot and have your front foot ready to move up to the top truck bolts position.

Here comes the hard part: place your front foot on the board and lean over the edge of the ramp, pushing down hard on the front of the board.

Stay level with the board – don't lean too far forwards or too far back.

The moment the board makes full contact with the ramp, bend your knees. This will stabilize you and bring you closer to the ground, so it won't hurt so much if you bail, and will enable you to pump out at the bottom of the ramp.

N.B. A good way to get over the fear is simply to take a deep breath and go for it!

ROCK 'N' ROLL **

As you ride up to the lip of the ramp, simply push your front foot down so that the board stalls, with your front wheels on the top standing bit of the ramp and your back wheels hanging off the end of the coping.

To get out of it, simply put pressure on the tail, bringing up the front end of the board, and lean back. Hopefully, you won't snag your trucks.

BLUNT TO FAKIE **

Ride up to the lip of the ramp and stall the board, so that your back wheels are sitting on the top of the coping (that's the blunt part).

Getting out of this stall is a little tricky. While in the blunt position, you should find there's still enough give in the tail for a little ollie.

Pop the tail to bring the rear wheels off the coping, and start to drop back in.

Make sure you keep your front wheels well clear of the coping before you put pressure on the front foot again, otherwise you may snag the trucks and wipe out.

FRONTSIDE GRIND ***

Get good speed up towards the top of the ramp.

Do a frontside turn, using your rear foot to slide the back end of the board up to the coping.

When your nose is clear of the coping and your rear wheels are level, stand up – this vertical action will push the board into a 50-50 grind.

Remember, grind too far and you'll fall off the edge of the ramp. To pull out of the grind, tilt the board so that the side wheels make contact with the ramp again.

Steer the board back into the ramp.

OLD SKOOL

Here are a few favourite old skool tricks:

BONELESS *

While going along, place your hand on the side of the board.

Take your front foot off the board and put it on the floor.

Jump with your front foot while keeping your back foot on the tail and holding on to the board.

While in the air, place your front foot back on the board and let go of the side of the board.

Land with legs bent and ride away.

THE MONKEY *

Place one foot on the tail and one on the nose.

Walk the board sideways by pivoting from nose to tail.

NO COMPLY *

Ride up to a small block in your path.

Take your front foot off the board and place it on the block.

Kick your tail down with your back foot to get a little air and push the board over the block at the same time.

When the board is just about to touch the ground on the other side of the block, put your front foot back on the board.

POGO **

Stand on the board, kick the tail down hard and move your front foot out of the way.

As the board stands up on its tail, step on to the top of the back truck and grab the nose of your board with your hand.

With the board gripped between your two feet, begin to hop up and down on your tail.

BONI-ONI **

While riding along, kick your tail down and, at the same time, take your front foot off the board and put it on the ground.

The nose of the board will shoot up.

Catch the nose of the board with your hand, then use your front foot to jump backside 180.

Land with both feet on the board.

SKATE SPEAK

Air short for aerial; simply getting all four wheels off the ground, usually off a ramp or kicker. The higher you are off the ground, the bigger the air

Alley-oop when making the transition from one ramp to another, you turn 180 degrees in the opposite direction from the way you are jumping

Axle the threaded bolt that runs through the truck that you put your wheels on

Axle nut the nut that holds the wheel in place on the axle

Axle slide when the axle sticks out more

on one side than the other; some trucks guarantee no slipping

Backside when you turn in the air with your back facing the ramp or obstacle; also when you run up to an obstacle on your heel-side of the board

Bail to stop halfway through a trick to avoid injury

Bank any incline where you can pull off a skating trick

Baseplate the main piece of metal on the truck that attaches to the deck

Bearing the reason your board runs smooth: a bunch of steel ball bearings encased in metal between the rubber of your wheels and the axle of the truck; you can buy different quality bearings and when they wear out, replace them

Bearing spacers washers that go between the two bearings on a wheel

Bitchslide to pull off a slide without ollieing

Bombing just going as fast as you can, usually down a hill

Burn the marks left by your wheels on the darkside of the deck

Bushing/Bushing cups the bushing are the rubbers above and beneath the hanger on the truck; the bushing cups are bowl-shaped washers that support them

Bust to pull off a trick successfully; if a place is a 'bust', then you're likely to get thrown out

Carve to skate in a long, curving arc

Catch to stop a trick in midair (usually at its highest point) and then to land it

Cess slide to slide sideways on all four wheels, best on slippery surfaces

Chip to break a small chunk of wood off your deck

Concave/Convex just like the hills in a geography lesson

Coping anything you attach to an object to make it easier to grind

Darkside the underside of your board

Deck the flat, wooden, standing surface of the skateboard

Demo usually put out on video by different skate companies or shops, in order to show off their pro skaters, new tricks and help sell their products

Dildo when a trick turns nasty and you land sitting on the nose or tail

Double two sets of steps separated by a flat surface

Drop-in when you start your run from the top of a ramp and ride down it

Durometer the device used to measure

the hardness of the polyurethane that the wheels are made of; a number ranging from 0 to 100 – soft wheels have a durometer of about 85, hard wheels are 97 or higher

Early grab grabbing the deck before you leave the ramp

Escalator a smooth man-made hill that usually runs alongside a set of steps; often found in skate parks

Fakie skating backwards – the skater is standing in a normal stance, but the board is moving backwards (not to be confused with 'switch stance')

Flatland flat skating without obstacles

Flatspots a worn-out section of the wheel – usually caused by doing too many powerslides!

Fliptrick any trick where the board spins on its axis (kickflips, heelflips, etc.)

Focus to break a board in half

Frontside a trick or turn where the front of the skater's body is facing the ramp or obstacle

Funbox any kind of box that you can do tricks on, often shaped like a pyramid with the top cut off

Gap jumpable space between objects

Goofy (foot) riding with the right foot

forward and left foot on the tail, the opposite of 'regular foot'

Grab the act of grabbing different parts of the board while making air

Grind any trick where you scrape, or grind, one or both axles on a curb, railing, or other surface

> **Crooked grind** grinding on only the front truck while sliding

> **50-50 grind** grinding on both trucks

> **Nosegrind** grinding on only the front truck

> **5-0 grind** grinding on only the back truck

Grip tape the sandpaper that you stick on your deck to keep you gripped to the board

Grommets little kid skaters

Halfpipe a U-shaped ramp of any size, usually with a flat section in the middle

Handrail a rail running next to a set of steps. Pedestrians use them to hold on to, but I'm sure you can come up with a better use

Hangup when your back truck gets caught on the coping off the halfpipe resulting in a wipeout

Hanger the large part of the truck that

the wheels connect to; also the area on which you grind

Hardware nuts and bolts

Hip two transitions back-to-back or a double-sided bank

Jetty a ledge next to a set of steps, that continues flat as the steps descend

Kingpin the steering bolt that also holds the two parts of the truck together

Kiss the expression is 'to kiss the rail'; when you just catch the end of the rail with a grind

Kinked rail a rail that has kinks in it, making it more difficult to grind or slide

Land to pull off a trick successfully

Late when you reach the peak of your ollie and then pull off the trick

Launch ramp/kicker a quarterpipe that doesn't go vertical, to help you get bigger airs

Ledge a grindable surface

Line pulling off several tricks in a row; also a set path through a skate park

Lip the edge of any trickable surface; usually grindable

Local someone who skates the spot regularly

Lock in stabilizing on a grind or slide

Manual basically a wheelie, just balancing on two wheels; a nose manual is balancing on the front two wheels

Mini ramp a baby halfpipe, around two to four feet high

Mongo (foot) pushing with your front foot, while your back foot is on the board

Mounting hardware the pins that attach the trucks to the deck

Mounting holes the holes drilled in the deck for the trucks to connect to

Nollie an ollie performed by tapping the nose of the board on the ground

Nose although most decks are symmetrical, you usually end up picking a front and a back; the front is your nose

Nosepick to stall on a ledge with just the nose of the board

Noseslide sliding the underside of the nose end of the board on a ledge or lip

Old skool tricks, skaters, clothes, vids, etc.; anything that is seen as outdated

Ollie a jump performed by tapping the tail of the board on the ground, which is the basis for almost every trick. It involves kicking down the tail and then using your front foot to level out the board

O-vert any transition that goes over vertical, so it is facing down

Ply the layers of wood that make up your board. Usually a deck is made of 7 or 8 layers of ply; the more layers, the stronger, but also the heavier

Pole riding up any bent pole sticking out of the ground

Pop you pop the tail in order to get air; also the amount of kick in the tail of the skateboard

Primo when your board is resting on its side

Pump the act of flexing your legs at the

right moment, in order to build up height and speed on the ramp

Push getting around, by using one foot to push yourself while on the board

Pyramid mostly found in skateparks and usually made of wood; a giant pyramid used to pull tricks on

Rad something cool; also the old skool magazine *RAD* (Read And Destroy)

Rail any grindable pole; also the edge of the skateboard and plastic strips attached to the board's underside

Railslide where the skater slides the underside of the deck along an object

Regular (foot) riding with the left foot forward and the right foot on the tail, the opposite of 'goofy (foot)'

Revert the 180 degree spin after completing a trick

Riser rubber plates that are fixed under the truck, which help protect the truck and stop rubs

Rub when the wheel catches the darkside of the deck, causing the skateboard to brake suddenly

Sack tap landing with your balls on the rail (Ouch!)

Session also known as a jam; when

skaters gather to skate a spot for a length of time

Sick an amazing trick

Skate camp summer camp for skaters, where you can meet other skaters, learn new tricks, etc.

Sketchy a dodgy trick; one that is only just pulled off

Slam a major fall

Slide when you slide on an obstacle with any part of the board

Snake a cross between a halfpipe and a small road around a skatepark

Spine the coping edge when you put two quarterpipes back-to-back

Sponsored when a company or shop gives you free products if you ride for them

Stall when you pull a trick into a sliding or grinding position, but you don't actually grind – you just balance

Stances the different ways you can stand on the board

Street skating skating in a public place, and using obstacles, such as kerbs, benches and handrails, to pull off tricks

Stress cracks cracks that appear around the truck mounting holes

Switch stance riding the board with the opposite footing from normal (see Goofy and Regular foot)

Tail the rear concave of your deck

Tailslide sliding the underside of the tail end of a board on a ledge or lip

Tech complex flatland tricks

Tic Tac an old skool move: getting forward motion by moving your nose from right to left

Top sheet top layer of wood on a board

Transfer any trick jumping from one obstacle to another

Transition the incline on a ramp

Trick any stunt on a skateboard

Tricked up a board with really good components on it

Trucks the big metal chunk screwed to the bottom of your deck used to steer and grind

Tweak to add your own personal touch to a trick

Vert short for vertical; skating on ramps and other vertical structures

Vert ramp a halfpipe, usually at least 8 feet tall, with steep sides that are vertical near the top

Wallie to ollie off a vertical wall

Wheelbase the distance between the front and back wheels, measured between the innermost truck holes

Wheels made of polyurethane, and sized between 39 and 66 mm in diameter